MW00624216

Griffin's Heart

Griffin's Heart

MOURNING YOUR PET WITH NO APOLOGIES

A MEMOIR,
HEALING JOURNAL,
and KEEPSAKE.

REAGAN J PASTERNAK

CREATURES ALIGN PRESS
LOS ANGELES

Creatures Align Press
14320 Ventura Blvd. #803
Los Angeles, CA 91423

For information about special discounts for bulk purchases, please
contact Creatures Align Press at hello@creaturesalignpress.com.
Creatures Align Press can bring the author to your live event. For
more information or to book an event, contact Creatures Align Press
at hello@creaturesalignpress.com.

ISBN 978-0-578-70446-3
Library of Congress Number Control Number: 2020910068

Cover art and book design by Kelcey Parker
Edited by Pam Alster-Jahrmakt, Nyei Murez, Daniel Johnson

Printed in China

First Printing

10 9 8 7 6 5 4 3 2 1

www.griffinsheart.com
www.creaturesalignpress.com

FSC
www.fsc.org
MIX
Paper from
responsible sources
FSC® C074709

For Griffin

I hope you're curled up with your sister somewhere
enjoying a soft serve ice-cream cone.

CONTENTS

PART II: ACTIVE REMEMBERING

PART III: TO SAY GOODBYE

Who do you dedicate this book to?

Your animal's name:

Nila aka "Nila-Roo" or "Roo"

"**Until one has loved an animal a part of one's soul remains unawakened.**"

~ Anatole France

How I Got Here

I had known Griffin was sick for almost a year before he died.

That year was torturous—almost unbearable actually. Daily pills, raw food diets, and pretty much every animal specialist in Los Angeles had their turn. But nothing was making him better. It was months and months of MRIs, vet trips, and credit card bills, while my poor cat was becoming short of breath and losing feeling in different limbs. Chopping up little white pills became the norm. He took those meds like a champ... at first. But by the end, he'd had enough. He would hear the pill bottle rattle and stare down at the floor, defeated. He was tired, he was fed up and I didn't blame him.

I'd wake up to see his tiny face and wonder if he'd make it through another day. He had become such a part of me—I couldn't really imagine what life would be like without him. I remember the twisting feeling in my chest as I shuffled to the bathroom one early morning. It was still dark but I could make out his funny little silhouette and his giant saucer eyes slow-blinking at me. I slumped over on the toilet and sobbed as he crawled over to my feet. He looked up at my face, letting out a tiny mew, as if to say, "Why so grim?" Because, I thought, I was going to lose my companion, my little soulmate. And it was sinking in.

And then, when it finally happened, I couldn't quite accept that he was actually gone. I'd had other animals. I'd experienced other deaths. But this pain was different somehow. It was sharp and confusing. It had a name all of its own and it seemed to follow me like a shadow.

Griffin was a Devon Rex. If you've ever seen that particular breed of cat, you'll know they appear much more like an alien-monkey hybrid than your typical feline. He was the color of an apricot with wrinkly skin and huge pale green eyes. His coat looked like crushed velvet and felt like cotton. Some people thought he was strange looking; I thought he was the most amazing creature I'd ever seen. Griffin had no hunting game whatsoever. In fact, when our dumpy one-bedroom apartment was invaded by rats, Griffin pretty much invited them in to hang out. He *befriended* the rats. He never hissed or scratched or bit even when he was in his gravest pain. He smelled like a beanbag and was unique and clever and kind. I loved that cat. He brought me pure joy, and also intense heartbreak.

After he died, I had people everywhere reminding me that this was just an *animal*, a pet.

"Animals don't live that long," the taxi driver said,

trying to console me as I quietly wept in the back of his car the day that Griffin died. "It's okay sweetheart, go get another one and you'll feel much better."

He meant well.

I decided, with the help from what I knew to be 'societal norms,' that it would be *appropriate* to hide the pain far, far away. So, I pushed the memories and anguish into the corners of my mind and photos or other reminders into the dark, dusty spaces of desk drawers.

Phewf.

I could pretend to be normal again.

Months went by. Life went on, of course. I actually did get another cat, a stray ginger who needed a home, and then a puppy from a local rescue. My house was filled with animals that needed to be loved. And they were loved in spades.

But the loss of Griffin was still everywhere.

Every so often the truth would whisper from those hiding spots. No matter what pretty bandaid I stuck over my heart, the wound remained right there. It was real.

And life was doing that thing that it sometimes does where it finds you at your weaker points and then throws a whole bunch of other complications your way to see if you can take it. Do you know what I'm talking about? Work, money, family—all of it at its ugliest, scrambled up and tossed into my world. "Here, catch this mess!" Well, I caught it. All of it. I just couldn't seem to figure out what to do with this collection of problems in my already shaky grasp. My nerves were shot. I felt lost and unlike myself. I was what you'd call *going through the motions*. Barely.

And worst of all, I couldn't sleep.

If you've ever experienced insomnia you'll understand the word "frustrating." No... FRUUUUSTRRRATINGGG!!!

You're tired beyond belief and yet you lie there watching the numbers on the clock flip forward. It's like time is mocking your impossible situation. Sleep deprivation becomes its own entity and you know there's nothing you can do to fight this wide awake monster. But you try. Oh you try, until you see the sun coming out and you can only hope that tonight will be different. And sometimes it is. Sometimes the right combination of herbs, or when I'm really desperate, over-the-counter sleep aids, does the trick.

Not this time.

So, with the urging of my worried husband, I went to see a doctor—a psychiatrist, to be frank. I had my own preconceived notions about this kind of treatment, but at this point I just knew I had to find my way back to sleep.

A friend had told me how the appointment would most likely go, that these were the kinds of doctors who would ask you to describe the problem, nod a couple times, scribble something on a little slip of paper, and send you on your way. Painless.

Well, the woman who met me at the door to her office did not fit that mold at all. She was immediately engaging and relatable. She was wise and centered with an intense focus that was now fixed upon me. I knew as soon as I introduced myself to her that I wasn't gonna get off that easy. She wanted to know my family history, my upbringing—the theme song to my own personal sob story. She asked detailed questions that required difficult, honest answers. I gave her an abbreviated, detached version. I mainly looked at my hands while I spoke. I assured her that I'd covered a lot of this "stuff" in therapy before, that I wasn't here to get into my rollercoaster ride of a childhood.

"What are you here for?" she said.

"I can't sleep," I said.

"But *why* can't you sleep?"

"Well, it's all that stuff I just told you. Just, you know, the family drama stuff and work, and also…"

"Yes?"

"Also my cat," I said. And this was when I began to break. "He died. He died, and I don't know what to do because I miss him so much." The mess was unfolding.

"What was his name?" she said.

"He was Griffin and he was my baby and my buddy and I really loved him and I know he was an animal but…" I couldn't finish.

"What color was he?"

"Orange… kind of. He had these huge ears," I said.

"How did he die?"

"Heart failure. He was only seven. He got sick somehow."

My doctor looked at me. She squinted her eyes.

"Hmmm, that's interesting," she said. "You know in some cultures, people believe that an animal will take on the burden or the disease of the person they love, to give them some relief from whatever hardship they might be carrying."

I stared at her.

"I just find it interesting, because it seems to me, in our short session, that you've had a lot of heartbreak in your life, from every angle, heartbreak. And this animal, this Griffin, who you clearly had some deep, perhaps spiritual connection with, ended up dying of a sick heart. Hmmm. Interesting."

And then she pulled out her little notepad and began to scribble.

"I will give you a prescription that should help you sleep," she said, "but it seems to me, you need to learn how to mourn your cat."

Just like that, the loss of my beloved pet had been taken seriously. By a *professional*. My pain had been validated with a few compassionate words. And I knew I had to learn to grieve. Properly.

That night I pulled out the printed photos of Griffin that I'd hidden deep inside my desk. I gave myself *permission* to miss him as I set them down beside me—a sweet stack of memories that I didn't have to ignore anymore. I was tired of faking it. Then, I took out my journal and I wrote. Man oh man, did I write. I wrote about everything that he'd been through with me in his seven-and-a-half-year life. The breakups, the moves, the triumphs and the many, many failures. I wrote about what he represented to me. He'd witnessed so much of my life. I wrote about the guilt and the pain and the joy. And then I wrote some more. It's hard to explain the feeling I had that night, journaling out all I'd been holding onto since losing him. But I knew that I was not clutching onto the pain quite as tightly when I was done. And the release felt honest. It felt *right*.

And whaddaya know? For the first time in over three months—I *slept*.

With each subsequent therapy session I was able to talk more freely. I realized that I had desperately needed someone to validate these feelings of loss—to legitimize my pain. I had tried to erase the animal that had shown me nothing but love, when instead he should have been remembered, celebrated even.

Throughout the years following Griffin's death, I dove into the idea of grief. Of mourning an animal. I *allowed* myself the *right*, the *privilege* of honoring his life. It took time and some very uncomfortable moments, but the true healing that evolved was worth it.

So, here I am. And now *I* am going to take *you* and *your* loss seriously. You are not alone in this difficult time. I will pass on any advice or helpful insights I've learned along this path of mourning Griffin. I will offer up the memoirs, eulogies, and tributes of others who have dealt with the loss of their own sweet animals.

Because they deserve to be remembered. They do.

They deserve to be honored, cherished, and mourned. And that's the most important part of what I've learned so far.

"Everyone grieves. Most have forgotten the art of mourning. Mourning is "going public" with your grief. Excavating the internal, and pushing it up and out. In a safe space. Mourning is a path to healing."

~ Tom Zuba, grief guide, author, speaker, and all-around inspirational human being

How to Use This Book

Every day, before I sat down to write *Griffin's Heart*, I cleared my mind and asked myself what my specific intention was in creating this book. What, ultimately, did I hope to accomplish? The answer was always the same. I wanted you (the reader) to feel like I was sitting on the couch with you (throw blankets optional) or at a cozy coffee shop (decaf after 2pm please). *Listening.* Commiserating a little. Letting you cry or vent as often as you needed. But also, gently nudging you toward the lighter part of yourself—the version of you that evolves after the death of someone you love.

And then when you have turned the last page, you will have created something of your own—a personalized keepsake full of precious memories, photos, and your own healing words that will both document and honor a very special life lived.

I'm offering up this book to serve as a friend who will wait patiently as you take all the time that you need to heal. I have shared my own deeply personal anecdotes in the hope that you, too, will allow yourself the space to be truly vulnerable. I want you to know that I am with you. Every word is sincerely from my heart to yours. Every page has been planned out with meticulous deliberation. My wish is that it will serve as a roadmap through your grief and that it will lead you to the other side as gracefully and full of love as possible.

Some tips on how to use this book:

- Before you start this journey, I urge you to print any photos you have of your animal. There are plenty of print places online if you're having trouble finding somewhere convenient to go. Use your printed photos in the spaces suggested as well as on any other page you like.

- I will give you thoughts to contemplate, and then space to write, or *unload* if you will, throughout this book. If at any point you do not feel it will serve you to write, or read for that matter, please don't. You can come back to it when the feeling is less "raw" or just skip it altogether.

- The time it takes to get through this book will be based on where you are in your grief process. Maybe you will finish the whole thing in one sitting. That's great! But maybe you'll need to keep it on the bedside table and read a page per day. Also good. Listen to yourself and stop when you've had enough. Go for a walk, distract yourself and let what you've read or wrote marinate. Things usually make more sense when we give them a little space.

- I do recommend sticking to the suggested order of sections. Each part feeds off of the one before it and was carefully placed where it is for a reason.

- There are a lot of breathing exercises! Breath is hindered by heartbreak so I'm gonna try to help you get back in touch with yours.

Some of the tools will be practical, others whimsical. Some are activities to access a different part of yourself and contribute to your healing as a whole. Try to keep an open mind and be kind to yourself. Always remember this book is for *you!* Make it work in whatever way you need it to. I want it to bring you comfort. And peace. And maybe even a tiny bit of closure.

This is the book I wish I'd had when *my* animal soulmate, my Griffin, died.

....

Share your animal's story with others who KNOW and RESPECT how you're feeling on our Instagram page @griffinsheartbook. Email your words and images to reagan@griffinsheart.com.

....

It is important to note that I am NOT a doctor. Not even close. The information used in this book is shared only because it made sense for me. It is meant to be motivational and provide helpful information on the subjects discussed. This book is not meant to be used, nor should it be, to diagnose or treat any medical condition.

GRIFFIN'S HEART

PART I

TO LOSE AN ANIMAL

"You can close the door on grief, but it will find a way to peek in through the window."

~ Unknown

Checking in...

Hey there. Big love to you.

When I started this book, my heart felt ripped up. I was raw and ridden with guilt.

And vet bills.

My insomnia was at an all-time high and I had no idea how to move forward.

Where are *you* emotionally today?

This is the beginning of your grief journey. Are you just here to gently explore the pathway of your healing? Would you rather use this book as a tool to help honor your pet so that they can be remembered in a deliberate way? Perhaps this book will be a way to free up any tangled emotions. Or for you to feel understood. Maybe you'll figure it out as you go along.

JOURNAL EXERCISE

Answer the questions posed on the previous page. Write down whatever truth comes up for you.

_____

_____

_____

_____

_____

_____

_____

_____

_____

_____

_____

_____

_____

Beings

The spiritual teacher Eckhart Tolle talks about a higher state of consciousness, or the *soul*, if you will. Some people might prefer the term "higher self" or "true self." Either way, Tolle is referring to that non-egoic part of ourselves that mirrors the vastness, the non-physical aspect of what makes us who we truly are.

He believes animals also share this consciousness, and that on this level we are not separate. In fact, we are here to help each other evolve.

At one of Mr. Tolle's events a man stood up to ask how he could move past the pain that was left behind when his beloved animal died. It was heartbreaking and all too familiar to watch this man apologetically express his profound sadness, making disclaimers that I have made myself when compelled to compare the loss of a pet to the loss of a human.

I took great comfort in watching Mr. Tolle talk to this man with genuine compassion. He explained that people who have not loved an animal will not understand, and that the connection between a pet and their human can be sacred. It is beyond language. It is of the soul or the "Being." In fact, when addressing this audience member's grief, Tolle called pets "Guardians of Being."

I love this so much. Pets can guard us physically, but perhaps more importantly, they keep us in touch with our deeper selves. They "guard" the part of us that gets lost so often in our cerebral interpretations of life and bring us back to the feeling of love and truth. This comes naturally to animals because they are pure "Being" themselves. They are without pretense, or ego.

So, for the duration of this book, I will often refer to our pets, the ones to whom we dedicate this journal and keepsake, as "Beings."

They may be dogs, or cats, birds, hamsters—yours could be a flying squirrel for all I know. You might refer to them as your "fur-baby," "buddy," or "sweetheart," but for the purposes of this book, I think "Being" sums it up perfectly.

Thank you, Eckhart Tolle.

When I think about Griffin's soul, his "Being," I feel a sweetness, an otherworldly kindness, and a sense of innocence. Remembering that *essence* allows me to feel connected to him again.

JOURNAL EXERCISE

Contemplate this quote, "The essence of anything is the thing that always stays true about them in any situation." This was said by the character, Sam Gardner in the television series, Atypical.

Can you put into words what you feel when you think about the essence of your Being?

_____

_____

_____

_____

_____

_____

_____

_____

_____

_____

Space for photo

"What we resist persists."

~ Carl Jung

Where Does the Pain Go?

I'm learning that the way out really is through.

We don't want to deal with the pain left behind by our Being's death. It's too uncomfortable. Too hard to explain to people. So we find distractions. We work ourselves silly, surround ourselves with all the shiny objects we can find and try to ignore that inconvenient heartbreak. And in time, our memory fades. And it may feel like we're finally moving on. But if we don't treat the ACTUAL problem, *where does the pain go?*

We humans are deeply conditioned to avoid emotional discomfort. A plethora of books and theories have been written about how our bodies overcompensate for unresolved (or subconscious) mental anguish—in this case, grief. A person's back goes out, or they get digestive problems. Maybe it will manifest as panic attacks, depression, anxiety, stress, you name it—all just clever ways for our brains to let us know that there is something going on that we need to deal with.

In my research, perhaps the most amazing finding was how medical literature supports the implication that intense, prolonged grief can have a negative effect on our cardiovascular health. We tend to think of heartbreak as more of a symbolic notion, but physical stress, such as the loss of a loved one, can result in an actual syndrome called Takotsubo Cardiomyopathy—otherwise known as *Broken Heart Syndrome*—where a weakening of the left ventricle is caused by this type of severe emotional stress.[2]

Proactive mourning is essential. Unprocessed life experiences stay in you and can pervade the way we handle events in the future. And in the process of mourning an animal, where many people can be dismissive of this brand of grief, we are in greater danger of shoving the pain away, or disguising it, often even from ourselves, so that it just becomes a heavy rock we carry around, unattended to.

The psychologist Carl Jung famously said, "What we resist not only persists but will grow in size." Denying, or *resisting*, your grief will not make it go away—in fact, it can cause it to become something more urgent. For me it was severe insomnia that led to back pain. But perhaps, if we can accept and even embrace these feelings of loss, we can allow an opportunity to learn and grow. And *heal*.

Journal It Out

Journaling is good for healing because it allows you to carry an idea or emotion to fruition. In today's world we're bombarded by technology and stimuli from every angle. It's tough to string a thought together before a buzzing or bleeping 'smart' device interrupts us and changes our mental direction. The demands of life are unrelenting, which can mean introspection and self care are scarce. We might have a flicker of a notion, but before we can find out what it is about, we push it away and are distracted by what's next. Thoughts are choppy and crowded and need to be tended to before they slip away.

This goes doubly for pushing away an emotion we perceive as negative or uncomfortable—a memory that might make us feel *too much*. The truth is, the best way to actually clear that energy is to explore it. Allow yourself to see it from all of its angles and hear the story it wants to tell your heart. Writing out thoughts is a mindful way to carve out that time to explore and unearth the feelings we are prone to bury. There may be difficult moments as you journal your experiences, especially when dealing with loss—I will do my best to guide you with cues—but you can also just choose to write in your own free-flow method instead. Take your time. Come back to it later if you need to. Just try to remember the feelings are temporary and dealing with them in this gentle way won't actually hurt you.

It can feel counterintuitive, I know—deliberately diving head first into the very emotion our brain is telling us to avoid. But surprisingly, when we do finally allow these feelings to breathe, even if it's just for a couple of minutes a day, the sharp edge of that hurt tends to dissipate. As if the pain is saying, "Thank you for acknowledging my existence—I've been heard!"

So, let's dive in together. I'm with you, my friend. Nobody will judge you here. You have lost a loved one and you can feel however you darn well want.

. . . .

Recommended reading: John E. Sarno, *The Divided Mind*. Wei-Ting Chang, Wen-Lieng Yu, Chon-Seng Hong, Chia-Te Liao, *Stress (Takotsubo) Cardiomyopathy: A Crosstalk between the Brain and the Heart*.

. . . .

EXERCISE

Sit quietly wherever you are right now. Close your eyes and imagine that you are smelling a beautiful rose. The idea behind smelling a rose is that it deepens and expands your breath in a far more productive way. Breathe in through your nose and out through your mouth. Try this five times. For now, just practice allowing any uncomfortable feelings to be there. This is your time to kindly accept these feelings and emotions—to respect them. It's a safe space to provide yourself some cathartic relief. When you know you are ready to end this exercise, try saying the mantra "Love will heal my wounds" a few times.

. . . . . .

JOURNAL EXERCISE

What thoughts or emotions came up for you after this exercise? Write it all down -- with no apologies.

_____

_____

_____

_____

_____

_____

_____

_____

_____

_____

_____

_____

_____

_____

The way out is through. It has been true for me, not just in dealing with the loss of Griffin, but in all aspects of my life. So, I'll keep saying it.

The
way
out
is
through

Sometimes we can locate where the pain resides in us physically. When Griffin died, my heart felt clenched. My chest became tight and my shoulders even tried to overcompensate by hunching forward a little.

EXERCISE

Can you feel which part of yourself the pain was most attached to? Your neck maybe? Throat?

_____

_____

_____

_____

_____

_____

_____

_____

_____

_____

_____

_____

_____

_____

Use the diagram below to mark the areas where you feel pain in your body. Use an "x" to indicate pain spots. Use more than one "x" in areas that are especially painful.

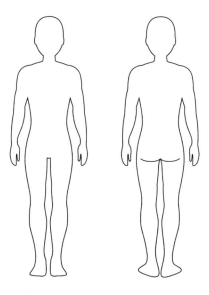

Now repeat the breathing exercise on page 45 with one small modification: Direct your breath to your specific pain spot or area of tension.

Disenfranchised Grief

Disenfranchised grief: grief that society (or some element of it) limits, does not expect, or may not allow a person to express. People who have lost an animal companion are often expected to keep their sorrow to themselves. Disenfranchised grief may isolate the bereaved individual from others and thus impede recovery. Also called **hidden grief**.

~ APA Dictionary Of Psychology

A few years ago I met a couple at the park. They were in their late sixties and were babysitting their granddaughter that day. I was with my son and our dog Jed. They were cooing over our sweet dog (yes, admiring our dog, not our son) and they began to open up about losing their own dog a couple of months earlier. Their sadness was palpable. I listened intently and told them I completely understood how they were feeling. They genuinely seemed shocked and relieved as they explained how their own grown children had been ridiculing them for holding onto their grief for so long.

I told them it had been years since Griffin died and that there was not an expiration date on grief, no matter the species. I encouraged them to take as long as they wanted, to honor and thank the pet who had clearly enriched their lives so much.

They reminded me why I needed to continue writing *Griffin's Heart.*

And I'm reminding you to surround yourself with people who understand, whether it be in person or on the Internet. Be careful who you share your grief with. Protect it and let it run its intentional course so that your healing is real.

....

Dr. Kenneth Doka, a Professor of Gerontology at the Graduate School of New Rochelle, first developed the concept of "disenfranchised grief". Learn more in Dr. Doka's book, *Disenfranchised Grief.*

....

EXERCISE

Try this: Wherever you are right now, close your eyes, and just let the pain be. Breathe into it. Maybe even thank it. It's reminding you that this anguish is real. It needs to be recognized and not forgotten. It will not be pushed aside so... we've gotta learn to work with it. That starts with non-judgmental acknowledgement.

Hello pain.

We're going to get through this together.

. . . .

JOURNAL EXERCISE

Journal out your thoughts after doing this exercise.

_____

_____

_____

_____

_____

_____

_____

_____

_____

_____

_____

_____

_____

_____

_____
_____
_____
_____
_____
_____
_____
_____
_____
_____
_____
_____
_____
_____
_____
_____
_____
_____
_____
_____

"We're talking about loss as the real or perceived deprivation of something one considers meaningful. If it's meaningful for me and I lose it, then it's loss, whether you think it is or not."

~ Keren Humphrey, counseling professor and author of *Counseling Strategies for Loss and Grief*

Some People Just Don't Get It...

When my sister's dog Bear died, she closed up. She wouldn't talk about it. She felt that no amount of words could ever express just how sad it was that this majestic animal, whose presence had filled the days with so much life and love, was no longer living. She also felt that people wouldn't or couldn't understand. While she stumbled through the first few days and weeks of mourning, she told friends and coworkers that there had been "a death in the family."

It's unfair to have to pretend, to feel the need to insinuate that this loss is something other than an animal in order for our grief to be taken seriously.

And yet, I remember some of the hurtful comments that I endured when speaking frankly after Griffin passed. It was exactly one day following Griffin's death and I was in a work meeting—I know, way too soon to be back to business as usual, but my practical mind told me to compartmentalize and keep moving forward with my career. I'm a professional, right? Well, my eyes were so red and puffy it looked like I'd had a serious fight with a can of pepper spray and my mind was still at home in bed, thinking I was lying there, staring at the ceiling. Nope. I was downtown, upright, in an important meeting surrounded by people who expected my A-game.

"I'm so sorry you guys, I know I look like a mess," I said to the four other people in the room. "My pet died yesterday and it's just hitting me pretty hard." The understatement of the year.

A polite mix of, "*Ohhhs*" and "*That's too bads*" filled the air.

And then a meeting attendee, I'll call him Ryan, said, "What was it? A cat or a dog?"

"He was a cat," I said.

"Oh." Ryan paused for a second and then said, "I'm a dog person."

Now, I guess this Ryan is a nice enough guy. Really, I mean no disrespect to him by quoting what I consider to be his unintentional insensitivity... but I couldn't help but wonder how he would have felt if I had, upon hearing the news that his aunt had died, said something to the effect of, "Oh, I'm more of an uncle person." Nobody in their right mind would dream of saying something like that about a human being. Now, in no way do I think animals and humans even *should* be compared, since every love and loss is entirely different. Ryan's empathy #fail was probably just that, a blunder. Death is awkward and I think we all sometimes struggle to find a way to relate through our own experience. Still, there it was—my beloved Griffin had been brushed off, sidelined into a sub-canine category of four-legged friends. And it hurt.

I'm an open book type of person. I share, and I'm not good at hiding my feelings. In fact, they are always there, right below the surface, ready to bubble up. And in my honesty after Griffin died, over and over again, I exposed myself to all forms of dismissiveness, insensitivity, and awkwardness. It had the unfortunate effect of making me feel more and more isolated. The fact that I was expected to just go about my everyday business, as though I should have "gotten over it" after one big cry, just wasn't going to cut it for me. I learned to be secretive about my bereavement, which I think in turn suppressed just how devastated I really was. I became, at times, defensive, and at other moments I wondered if I must be crazy for hurting so much.

Later that year, I read a popular self-help book in hopes of figuring myself out a bit more, of gaining some self-awareness and enlightenment. Sure enough, the book was filled with boatloads of well-conceived wisdom, but I stopped dead in my tracks when I came across a section on "love." The author postulates that the love a person feels for a pet is not real love; he says that love is an action, not a feeling. This author argues that the feeling a human has for their pet is only based on the immediate and conditional satisfaction when the animal's will coincides with ours.

Huh? Is love so cerebral? Could love be so

academically described?

I thought of the love I have for my husband, my childhood best girlfriend, for my parents and siblings.

For Griffin.

All different. All unmistakably real.

I was confused. How could this famous author, a PhD no less, be so wrong about love? But then the answer came to me in a way that was both gentle and crystal clear. The man who had written this mostly brilliant book quite simply could have never been blessed with the love of an animal. Maybe it was beyond his heart's capacity. Perhaps it just wasn't in the cards for him. I remember feeling a pang of sorrow for this author. I became acutely aware that some people may never get the chance to experience the incredibly pure and intimate love of an animal. How truly sad for them.

So, what can we learn from this? What's the takeaway? The action item? Quite simply put, it's that "some people just don't get it." It's unavoidable. *It's only how we respond that matters.*

And, my sister was being honest when she told people there had been a death in the fam'''ily after Bear died. Because when you love your Being the way she loved hers, they are indeed your family—often closer than any other member—and nothing less. It's on us to develop the skills to avoid further injury when we encounter those who do not understand. I believe that if we consciously acknowledge these statements as being born out of awkwardness—or perhaps because the person has never known the true love of a pet—then we can understand that this person is not qualified to judge or give advice during this excruciating time of loss.

Grief specialist Marty Tously says, *"I think it boils down to this: When dealing with others who aren't living up to our expectations of how we think they should "be there" for us, we have three choices: We can choose to bear with such people and simply ignore their shortcomings; we can assume a teacher's role and enlighten them about what we've learned about grief and what we need from them; or we can look to others who are more understanding to find the support we need and deserve."*

....

Marty Tousley is a bereavement counselor who specializes in human and pet loss. Visit griefhealing.com to learn more about her work.

....

SAY WHAT???

Suggested responses for when you may be confronted by insensitive comments:

THEY SAY:
"Ok, but it was just an animal. I mean, it's not the same as when a *human* dies."

CHEEKY INTERNAL VOICE SAYS:
"Is it the same as when a person says the dumbest thing ever? Because that's you. You just said the

dumbest thing I've ever heard."

INSTEAD:
Take a breath. Remind yourself that your feelings are valid. Your pain is real. This is probably not the right person to share your grief with, and it is not your job to educate them on the topic. Try redirecting the conversation to something else like "How was your meeting last week?" or "Oops, I think my Uber is here!" Go find someone who is safe to talk to about your grief, or pick up this book and remind yourself that you are not alone.

THEY SAY:
"Oh, I hate cats."

CHEEKY INTERNAL VOICE SAYS:
"Funny, my cat would have hated you too."

INSTEAD:
Take a breath. This is definitely someone who just doesn't get it. Redirect the conversation and/or look for the nearest exit. Protect your pain. You deserve better.

THEY SAY:
"Aren't you over that yet?"

CHEEKY INTERNAL VOICE SAYS:
"No, but I'm over you."

INSTEAD:
You can try saying "No. I'm really not. I guess grief has

no timeline or boundaries." Then you can resort to the old stand-by—*redirect the conversation*—"I better go clear out my junk mail. Gotta run!"

Nobody will completely understand the bond you shared with your Being. Nobody will know exactly what your specific pain feels like. How could they? Grief, in general, makes society uncomfortable. If we assume that people are well-meaning, even though their words may sound utterly clueless, then we are able to grant them grace and move on from hurtful comments more quickly. Don't get me wrong, we can *think* the comical, snarky response—humor is a cathartic release—but then take a breath and choose a peaceful path instead, which is often just a conscious redirect of the conversation. This will help you avoid tension with the offender in future interactions. Mindfulness in these situations goes a long way.

JOURNAL EXERCISE

How have things been with your family since your Being passed away?

_____

_____

_____

With your friends?

_____

_____

_____

With your work colleagues and associates?

_____

_____

_____

Have you felt, in any way, a need to "play down" the pain?

_____

_____

_____

Have you felt resentment for feeling like you have to make disclaimers?

_____

_____

_____

What do you wish someone would say or do?

_____

_____

_____

_____

_____

"An experience of collective pain does not deliver us from grief or sadness; it is a ministry of presence. These moments remind us that we are not alone in our darkness and that our broken heart is connected to every heart that has known pain since the beginning of time."

~ Brene Brown, *Braving the Wilderness: The Quest for True Belonging and the Courage to Stand Alone*

And Some People Do...

And then, thank goodness, there are the people who actually do understand. It will be their kind words and gestures that you will remember forever. They may be the ones who help carry you through, often without even knowing how much their empathy and thoughtfulness has impacted you.

Even if you do not feel safe enough to grieve openly with anyone you know directly—know that you are still not alone. There is an attractive anonymity in participating in online support groups where each person is seeking the same thing as you—a non-judgmental safe space to actively mourn. A study in the *Journal of Mental Health Counseling* had 38% of their subjects ranking their pet as their closest family member. You may not know them yet, but there are people out there who need you just as much as you may need them.

Editor Joe Yonan wrote an article in the *Washington Post* called "The Death of a Pet Can Hurt as Much as the Death of a Relative." In it he says, *"I'm no stranger to death. I was a mess of anger and confusion when my father, suffering the aftermath of a stroke, took his last gasps one day in 1995, his children gathered around his hospital bed. And three years later, the death of my sweet, beloved sister Bonny after a withering battle with brain cancer was nothing short of heartbreaking. Yet somehow, and much to my distress, **the death of my dog seems even harder**. I haven't felt grief quite like this since, well, the death of my previous dog five years ago."*

For me, learning that I was not alone in my anguish was an awakening.

I try to make an effort to remember all the evidence of compassion, of certain people's warmth, after Griffin died. An old friend I hadn't heard from in years reached out when she heard the news. Her gesture meant the world to me. I can recall running into an acquaintance at a meeting, and since it had been less than a week since Griffin's passing I was noticeably not doing my best. This girl took me aside and could not have been more lovely and helpful. And then there is the wonderful man who is now my husband, who took about twenty of my favorite pictures of Griffin and had them framed and mounted. They were hanging all over my bedroom wall one day when I got home.

Try not to isolate yourself. I completely understand the difficulty with rational thinking when you are in tremendous grief—I really do—and sometimes what we need is proper time to naturally go through our painful emotions. But when that time period goes on more than a few weeks, we must accept the help and support of those caring people who are worried about us. Long-standing withdrawal can lead to serious depression. If this becomes the case for you, please do not hesitate in getting professional help.

JOURNAL EXERCISE

Did you reach out to someone who helped you? What did they do or say?

_____

_____

_____

_____

_____

_____

_____

_____

Is there someone you can reach out to now, a friend, a coun-selor who can help?

_____

_____

_____

Space for photo

"**Women are called a "crazy cat lady" for having cats, but don't forget a man wrote an entire f**king musical about them.**"

~ Eden Dranger, writer,
comedian (@edendranger)

Crazy Cat Lady And Proud

There is no doubt that some people think I'm crazy for the way I have loved my animals, for how sad I was when I lost one of them. There are probably some who think I'm crazy for writing this book.

To those people I say, it's perfectly fine if you think I'm a crazy cat lady, or I need to "get a grip," or "it was just an animal." Because truthfully, I feel lucky and perhaps even special to have known such a precious and fulfilling love. I actually feel sad for anyone who has not. Because the love of an animal has an almost magical quality to it. And I refuse to apologize for the need to mourn that kind of loss.

If that makes me crazy then I don't wanna be sane. So there.

JOURNAL EXERCISE

Own it. Get out your crazy here, whatever that means to you.

_____

_____

_____

_____

_____

_____

_____

_____

_____

_____

_____

_____

_____

_____

_____

Space for photo

"My capacity for compassion is not species-specific."

~ Karen Dawn, animal rights and welfare advocate, and author of *Thanking The Monkey: Rethinking the Way We Treat Animals*

In Defense Of Compassion

About ten years ago I attended an event at a farm sanctuary in Southern California. I had no idea what to expect as I entered this sprawling twenty-six acre shelter filled with rescued cows, pigs, turkeys, and other farm animals, but when I left I was forever changed. I felt like the Grinch from the Dr. Seuss book, whose heart grew three sizes in one day. I heard the story of each animal's struggle, and ultimate *survival*—and my eyes became permanently open to the individuality of each and every life. How we all want the same things: to be loved, to feel safe, and to live.

I'll never forget one of the guest speakers who got in front of the crowd that day. Her name was Karen Dawn. She had wild, dark curly hair and spoke with a slight Australian accent while she looked at the audience with mesmerizing resolve. I would soon learn that she was a tireless hero in the world of animal rights, and her mission to change the way we think about animals continues to make me want to be a better person to this day.

A man in the audience raised his hand to ask his question. "How do you justify devoting so much of your time and resources to animals when there are actual *people* who are suffering? *Human beings* who are caught in natural disasters and war?"

Ms. Dawn took a deep breath that seemed to say she'd been faced with questions like these before. She replied, "Do you think that because I'm fighting for animals that it means I don't have room for empathy for anyone else? That I don't also care deeply for children or any other vulnerable people who are in need?"

And then she said the words that have stayed with me for all these years since hearing them: "My capacity for compassion is not species-specific."

So simple, so obvious, but also so profoundly important.

Perhaps if we can open our minds to the idea that we can be limitless in our compassion—that we can actually care about people *and* animals *and* the planet's wellbeing and still have room for so much more love; maybe then we'll discover what kind of superpowers we actually possess. How much we can truly help each other.

Grieving for an animal does not mean I don't cry when I see a news story about a tragic accident, or that I wasn't completely devastated by the loss of a close friend this year. It just means that my heart is capable of all kinds of love and I will mourn the loss of each one as needed in order to heal.

"The ones that love us, never really leave us."

~ Sirius Black, *Harry Potter and the Prisoner of Azkaban*

PART II

ACTIVE
REMEMBERING

"There is a beginning and an ending for everything that is alive. In between is living."

~ Bryan Mellonie and Robert Ingpen, *Lifetimes*

Memories

The living is in between. As hard as it feels right now, that's the part that really matters—where the simple memories we need to hold onto are made—like meandering walks in the park, sweet snuggles on the couch, and overly enthusiastic greetings at the door. It may sound obvious but that's what life is truly about—living and loving to the fullest, the part in between the beginning and the end.

Animals have a natural ability to do that, don't they? To live and love so completely. Throughout this book, it's my hope that you'll begin to unload the painful memories and then, through the exercises, reinforce the good. Because the "good" is the reason you're hurting from the loss. The good, is actually everything.

JOURNAL EXERCISE

Can you write about a favorite memory?

_____

_____

_____

_____

_____

_____

_____

_____

_____

_____

_____

_____

_____

_____

_____

Space for photo

The First Time Ever I Saw Your Face

When Griffin came into my life, I was a bit of a hot mess. I was in the beginning of what would become a tumultuous breakup with my first long-term boyfriend and I had just landed my first real job since leaving college. I was working sixteen-hour days and had no time to deal with, well, anything else. I was living on adrenaline and potato chips.

And way too much wine.

My boyfriend was intensely allergic to cats but we'd heard of a special breed that apparently didn't shed and was perfect for people with allergies. So, that year we got our first baby, a grouchy yet adorable black Devon Rex we called 'Cleo.' Cleo was tiny but chubby since birth. She was extremely discerning with whom she'd allow the privilege of enjoying her company but she loved her momma and would curl up on my shoulder for hours and purr her little face off.

Because of my long hours at work, I wanted Cleo to

have a companion to play with. I still don't know where or how we found Griffin's breeder, and now I shudder to think of what shady operation he came from. All I remember is that he was dropped off by a delivery truck sometime in the late evening while I was still at work. Sounds charming doesn't it? Adopt, don't shop, people! But I digress.

I'll never forget the call to tell me Griffin had arrived. I answered my flip phone to the sound of my boyfriend's laughter. He said, "Wait till you see him. He's awesome."

I was confused and said, "Hold on, why are you laughing? Hello?"

When I got home I understood.

I unlocked the door to our downtown Toronto apartment to see his little face. I, too, began to chuckle. "Wait. Are you sure this is right? Where is... his *fur*?" I said. "Why are his ears so... I mean, they're *giant*."

Griffin pranced over to me as if he already owned the place and let out a scratchy meow that seemed to say, "What took you so long?"

I was in love.

It turns out, this is what normal Devon Rex's are like: coated in velvety peach fuzz with huge eyes and ears. Cleo was the unusual one, bred with more fur.

I had to get on a flight first thing the next morning but I stayed up and stared at this little near-hairless wonder purring right beside me all night. I remember missing him the whole time I was away.

He brought instant joy to a home that had lacked it

for months. And when my inevitable break-up happened, those two cats were my little lights through it all.

Every so often I recall the memory of Griffin's arrival and it always puts a huge smile on my face.

Personal Note:

I would like to say that I was embarrassingly naive and even ignorant about breeders when all this happened. I have since become a huge advocate for adopting pets from rescues and/ or dire situations. I am the proud owner of five much loved rescue animals as I write this today.

~ Reagan

JOURNAL EXERCISE

Can you write the story of how your Being came into your life? Do you remember your first thoughts and feelings? Or what stage you were at personally? Photos are welcome.

_____

_____

_____

_____

_____

_____

_____

_____

_____

_____

_____

_____

_____

Space for photo

Remembering the Physical Being

It's almost tragic how fickle and fragile our memory can be. In just a few weeks or months we begin to forget how our Being felt. I mean this literally: the fur (or feathers), nudges from wet noses (or beaks!), crackly paw pads, bent whiskers and all the parts of the physical being that we knew so well. In time, we have to settle for only describing sensations that were once so familiar.

Maybe forgetting is our body's coping mechanism so that we don't remain stuck in the past. For me though, I didn't want those beautiful sense memories to fade or vanish completely. The best parts of life are experienced through our senses and it can bring comfort and joy to remember the specific details. It can help to keep the picture we hold in our mind more complete. Because I wrote down Griffin's physical attributes so completely, all I have to do is read them and I can instantly remember every detail even now, years later. And that feels nice.

JOURNAL EXERCISE

Was your Being soft or scruffy? Silky smooth or bristly like a boot brush? Take a minute to remember what it was like to scratch and pet and bathe and groom.

_____

_____

_____

_____

_____

_____

What other physical features did you love? Think stinky breath, flabby belly pouches, and wonky dew claws.

_____

_____

_____

_____

Space for photo

Bittersweet Routine

I used to come home and be greeted.
I always took him for a walk at sunset.
There was so much noise in my home and now it
feels so quiet.

The void that opens up after the death of our Being can leave us feeling lost, like half a person. Once-familiar sounds—mews, woofs, purrs, chirps, and chortles—get replaced by silence.

It takes just a few days to realize how well-trained we really are by our Beings. Conditioned to prepare food on time, deliver treats on demand, open any and all closed doors, brush out matts, trim toenails, wash, cut, and the list goes on. We even become experts in collecting poop. And let's be honest, no matter how cute your little frou-frou was, poop is poop. It's warm and brown and stinky. And yet there we always were without hesitation, ready to scoop or bag or what-have-you all over again. Love is a powerful thing ain't it?

But now we go through the day without those familiar punctuation marks. We're no longer needed and the time, space, and quiet are all constant reminders. A broken routine on top of a broken heart is a double whammy and it can be overwhelming. Plain and simple.

So, let's just remember for a moment how our Beings shaped us. How they changed our lives each and every day. The neat tricks they taught us. The lengths we would go to in order to satisfy their bizarre needs. How we'd shuffle priorities and make ourselves late and lose sleep for them.

JOURNAL EXERCISE

The sweetest part of our days were...

_____

_____

_____

_____

_____

_____

_____

_____

Bedtime rituals? Sleep on the bed?

_____

_____

_____

_____

Mornings went like this... Woken up?

_____

_____

_____

_____

We always...

_____

_____

_____

_____

The part of our days I miss the most is...

_____

_____

_____

_____

Space for photo

Missing your Being is normal. It makes sense. But while we are healing, it's important to find productive ways to fill these empty spaces. For example, continue to get up and go for your morning walk, but perhaps listen to a podcast or some new music. Make sure you have a great book beside your bed or find a sleep meditation to form new nighttime rituals. Give back by fostering a pet in need. These are ways that you are *actively choosing* new habits as opposed to running away from the pain.

"Over the course of thirteen years, for instance, the same thing would happen with Gromit every morning. I would sit on my bed to put on my shoes, and he would drape himself across my lap. I would scratch his butt and he would reward me with a big sloppy kiss. Recently, I did the math: Accounting for the times I was traveling without him, this interaction happened more than 4,000 times. So it makes sense that when he died, it was months before I could touch my shoelaces without expecting to also touch him. And I had no idea what to do with my mornings without my pooch to require that small gesture of me."

~ Joe Yonan, "The Death of a Pet Can Hurt as Much as the Death of a Relative", via *The Washington Post*

Quirks and Idiosyncrasies

Griffin was a weird little dude. He'd gaze at me with eyes that said he was not of this world. If the cliche is that cats are supposed to be indifferent or aloof, then Griffin "didn't get the memo." Road trips were a breeze because he was as chill as any Golden Retriever I'd ever met. At the vet, while other cats sat nervously in their carriers, Griffin just observed quietly from my lap. He had a leash for walks and I would get double takes from strangers daily. I taught him to "sit" and "give a paw" like a dog. He preferred to drink his water from bottle caps and ate his food like no other animal I've ever owned—with one paw he'd delicately pick one nubbly out of the food bowl and bring his paw to his mouth and gently nibble the piece before crunching. The whole operation was as meticulous as it was ridiculous. We'd laugh out-loud sometimes watching him do it and it was a source of daily amusement that always brightened our moods.

It's those funny little quirks and idiosyncrasies that

are most endearing. They make us laugh, that most healthful of human behaviors.

JOURNAL EXERCISE

Remember a funny, eccentric, inexplicable behavior that brought you joy.

_____

_____

_____

_____

_____

_____

_____

_____

_____

_____

_____

_____

_____

How Your Being Got Her/His Name

There are two cats and three dogs that grace my home as I write this book. There's a story behind each of their names, some more elaborate than others, that gives a little bit of extra meaning to who they are to us.

When you first give an animal a name, there's that awkward week when you test it out and try to get used to it, before it sticks. Over time though, they all seem to grow into their names and somehow even 'own' any assigned backstories. Before long you cannot imagine any of them being called anything else.

Our animals names are:

Jed — He's our white fluffy dog who got his name from the song "Jed The Humanoid" by the band Granddaddy. This song made us think of Griffin a lot, so it was a tribute to him. (More on this in "Music Therapy")

Murmur — Murmur is an orange tabby who was

named after Griffin's heart murmur.

Luna — The tiny almond-eyed mutt who stole my son's heart. The first night we had her, our son, who was three at the time, held her on his lap and declared her name would be "Luna, after the full moon." It could not suit her more.

Doctor Purrpurr — Our Siamese kitty who I named after a famous forensic pathologist whose name is Dr. Joshua Perper (I'm a true crime nerd). We find this hilarious.

Stella — Our Great Pyrenees rescue. Our son decided he loved the name. And since "Luna" means the moon and "Stella" means the stars it just seemed... cosmic.

My husband Kelcey's soulmate animal was a Bernese Mountain dog named "Milo" who I never got to meet. Somehow I've always felt a strange connection to this incredible Being. And I love the story behind how he got his name.

Milo Aukerman Was a Dog
by Kelcey Parker

Coffee. Girls. Food. Possibly not in that order. Milo Aukerman was (and still is) the spectacled frontman for the legendary punk band The Descendents. Back in the 80s he belted out songs like "Clean Sheets" and "I'm Not a Loser" and "Hürtin' Crüe" all while sipping 'bonus cups' and not giving a f**k. To an awkward, pubescent kid on the East Coast of Canada, it was somehow... epic.

But it was more than that. Those words got me through my teenage years. Truly. Milo made it OK to not be "cool." He explained the basics of how the female of the species worked and got me excited about the prospect of visiting a Wienerschnitzel one day, which I finally did in the winter of Grade 12. High school was bad, college was worse, but Milo's words were constant and comforting.

Years later, in my thirties, a girlfriend (who was on her way out) encouraged me to buy a two-month-old Bernese Mountain Dog from the local pet store. She left and the dog stayed. My girlfriend could tell I was slipping deeper into a dark period of my life and she wasn't going to be the one to save me. So, there we were—a depressed, thirty-something college dropout/surf bum and a clumsy poof-ball that needed help with just about everything. I named him 'Milo' and we became inseparable. He came to work with me. He waited on the beach and chewed up seagull carcasses while I surfed. We hiked lake trails in the winter and he drank and drank and drank and drank, slurping up the murky lake water for minutes at a time. Which, I came to understand, was not a good sign.

A trip to the vet at around five months old revealed that Milo was born without fully formed kidneys—a birth defect commonly produced by puppy mills. How could this be? We were best buds and I had our lives together already planned out—chasing girls, coffee, and Mexican food with as many lake hikes and beach days as he wanted. And now, he had less than a year to live. There's no single word that could describe my state of mind during the next few months—but devastated, denial, anger, heartsick, all come to mind. One word however, does stand out above the rest—love. He gave it to me in spades and I returned it by the bucket load.

At nine months old, on the first day I had ever spent apart from Milo, he was hit by a car and killed. He had slipped away from his dog sitters via an unlatched back door and followed my scent down the driveway— but only part-way across the little two-lane highway to our boat launch. The last thing I had said to him before I turned and walked away for an afternoon of sailing that day was "Goodbye Milo, goodbye forever." I gave him a big hug and scratch and shook his muzzle. It was such a strange thing to say and I remember feeling weirded out by my own words. I also took a picture of him with my point-and-shoot. It was like the universe was pulling my strings so I could act out and document an awkward goodbye—one I didn't yet know would be so final.

So, the silver lining in this story is that Milo never suffered. Renal failure is brutal. You are basically poisoned by your own body. In his short nine months of life he was never sick and for that I am grateful. But if you haven't figured it out yet, this story isn't about silver linings, it's about salvation. Oblivious to his prognosis, Milo gave me the love I needed so much. I didn't sink into a deep depression. I didn't implode.

Instead, he taught me how precious every moment is with someone you love. He taught me to be a caregiver. To value your time on this planet. Life lessons I need to remind myself of even now almost fifteen years later. Thank you, Milo Aukerman for getting me through those angst-ridden teenage years. And thank you Milo for brightening that dark year in my thirties and for the downward spiral that never was—because of you. I hope you are drinking from a shimmering silver lake up there somewhere. And not too much. Miss you, pal.

....

Go to our Instagram page @griffinsheartbook to see pictures of Milo the Bernese Mountain dog.

....

I met my husband just two short weeks after his dog, Milo, had died. He had been so shattered by the loss that he hadn't brought himself to talk about it to anyone yet—but for some reason he told me. It was the first meaningful moment we shared and the seed for what was to come. My husband's love for his dog was a big part of why I fell for him in the first place. In fact, Kelcey even thanked Milo tearfully in our wedding vows. And so, when our first and only child was born, naming him after that sweet Bernese Mountain Dog—whose life had been cut way too short—was an easy decision to make. And yes, we do get funny looks from people sometimes when they find out that we named our *human* son after a dog, but hey—this is us, we love our animals.

JOURNAL EXERCISE

How did your Being get his/her name?

_____

_____

_____

_____

_____

_____

_____

_____

_____

_____

_____

_____

_____

_____

_____

Space for photo

"Many people only dream of angels. People who have pets are touched by angels every day."

~ Unknown

Necessary Angels

In so many ways our Beings look after us. They can provide meaningful emotional support—somehow knowing when and how to bring comfort when we're sad or distressed. They have an ability to say "It's OK. I'm here. And it's gonna be fine," without uttering a word. They are pure of heart. Even the grouchiest of them.

People often jump to the conclusion that someone this hurt over an animal's passing could not have experienced much pain in their life. Or loss. Well, that was certainly not the case with me. Perhaps this is the very thing that makes our pets so important to us, that they come in and give a type of reprieve to all the sadness.

I never had much formal religion in my life (*I will talk about this further in the section called Afterlife*), so the idea that angels fly down from heaven or appear in a Denny's pancake to blind you with heavenly awesomeness never made sense to me. But there are countless real, verifiable stories of animals protecting humans from attackers, sniffing out cancers, or warning us of danger from natural disasters. Performing 'divine' interventions, if you like. Every day they can be found helping the disabled or bringing joy and comfort to children in hospitals—and on and on.

I now believe that animals *are* our angels. Our angels here on Earth.

For me, Griffin represented *unconditional acceptance*—something I never really felt growing up. He provided constant comfort, even in my saddest moments. He was my first living responsibility as an adult and he made me feel less alone. He was indeed my 'necessary angel,' showing me that there can always be light, even in the darkest corridors. I needed to know that.

JOURNAL EXERCISE

Consider the idea of our pets as angels within the context of whatever you believe. Does it ring true for you and your Being? If it does, describe all of the ways your Being looked after you.

_____

_____

_____

_____

_____

Is it possible that your Being is still looking after you even after they have departed? What does that mean to you? Is it a comforting thought?

_____

_____

_____

_____

Erin's Angel, "Pumpkin"

by Erin Karpluk

I remember when I first laid eyes on Pumpkin. She was the first in her litter to run up to me, I cradled her in my arms and she began to purr. It was love at first sight. She stared up at me softly with her green eyes and I proudly proclaimed, "This is the one!" I remember feeling like the most magical gift ever had been given to me. I loved her immediately and vowed to make the best life for her.

Pumpkin and I became inseparable. I used to dress her up in Cabbage Patch Doll dresses, tuck her into my barbie bed, and carry her around the house with me everywhere I went. She was never fussed and slept with me every night. But my feline utopia couldn't last forever.

Over the next few years I became aware that my parents were fighting. I would regularly hear their muffled voices from my room and I was acutely aware of the increasingly hostile tone of their fights. I became obsessed with needing to know what they were talking about... plotting ways I might somehow diffuse a fight. Quietly I would tiptoe halfway down the stairs so I was able to hear. I can't recall how many hours, months, years I did this, sitting quietly on the stairs listening, stifling whimpers as huge teardrops spilled off my cheeks. Pumpkin would ALWAYS come to me during these times. She'd look up at me with her big green eyes, make soft concerned purr-meows (you know the ones?) as she examined my pained face and licked the tears from my cheeks. I would often hug her tightly and cry into her soft fur. She never flinched. She never left my side.

When Pumpkin died I was away in Saskatchewan for a swim meet. By this time my parents were separating. I have only seen my dad cry three times in his life. The first was when he had to break the news to me of Pumpkin's passing. It was my first experience with death and still the hardest I've been through in my life. I did not talk to my friends for weeks. I just stared out into the garden from my window.

In my early twenties I began seeing a Therapist. We spent a lot of time focusing on that time in my life and those hours spent on the stairs. It wasn't until I looked back with adult eyes that I realized Pumpkin was brought into my life for a very specific reason. She was not just a cat, she was my guardian angel. I believe this as truly as the earth is round, with every fiber of my being. I am so incredibly grateful for this beautiful angel who came and gave me the love and strength and comfort to get through the most traumatic event of my childhood. Had it not been for her, I would not be the same person I am today. Pumpkin, I thank you from the bottom of my heart and every part of my soul. I will love you forever and know you are with me always, my little fur-angel.

....

The complete version of Erin's story can be found on our Instagram page @griffinsheartbook.

....

"I have lived with several Zen masters—all of them cats."

~ Eckhart Tolle

Meditation For Healing

So *how* exactly can we get to this place of acceptance in our minds and hearts? For me, learning to meditate was the most peaceful and effective path to gradual healing. It granted me permission to immerse myself in my feelings privately and in manageable increments.

Learning how to *focus, command,* and *slow down* your breath is like a naturally occurring, free, and accessible miracle drug for our physical and emotional health. If you don't believe me, then just ask the next two-hundred-year-old tortoise you run into. Those peaceful reptiles seem to be the masters of meditation. They are breathing deeper and living way, way longer. Luckily, we can watch and learn.

When we use controlled, deep breathing, (à la our tortoise friends) we can slow down our heart rate and allow our nervous system to have a much needed break. We are better able to *allow* feelings and thoughts to come and go without being reactive to them. Just focusing on our breath can surprisingly teach us so much.

But the act of sitting and breathing can be both simple and, well, not so simple.

Grief can take a toll on your breath. I distinctly remember the shallowness of my breathing for months after Griffin died. It was as if glass had shattered in my heart and lungs. But I kept hearing about the countless benefits that come from incorporating a meditation practice into your daily routine. I was desperate to feel better, so I took it upon myself to explore my meditation options. I can say now that it may have been the single most important part of my grief journey. It was the baseline for everything else that followed. Once you get the hang of it, you can begin to incorporate some form or another of meditation into most other aspects of your life—and your healing. The slow and steady tortoise really can win the race.

In meditating for the specific purpose of grief, what worked best for me was the practice of "allowing." I would sit somewhere quietly every single day, whether I felt like it or not, and set my timer for ten minutes. I would breathe in and out and *observe* how each breath made me feel. A lot of the time it would make me feel pretty crummy. Or overwhelmed. Or soothed. However I felt, I would sit and breathe until I got better and better at *allowing* those feelings to come and go, without judgement, without fearing that I would cry—and often I would— because I knew my whole self needed to be able to feel these feelings in order to release them.

That said, meditation for grief doesn't always have to be done sitting crossed-legged on the floor. It can be taking a walk, looking at a picture, listening to a song, or reading a poem—whatever allows you to feel the truth of your pain and then breathing through it.

TIPS

Here are two tips that helped me when I was having trouble getting into the "meditative zone."

1. Often when we're in emotional distress, our breath can get trapped in our throat, making deep breathing tricky. When this happens, see if you can mentally force the breath into the abdomen, as if you were pushing a piece of food down through your neck and into your lower belly. Take this inhale to the count of four. Hold for two beats and then slowly exhale for a count of five. You can try this for a couple of minutes at first and then work your way up to longer durations.

2. I like reciting the phrase "All is well" three to five times before I start my breathing. I find these words soothing and centering.

....

Visit the Griffin's Heart YouTube channel to find guided meditations and breathing exercises.

....

Each day, little by little you can test the waters to know how much you are ready to accept, how ready you are to open up your heart again. Our breath is sometimes the best way we can measure how far we've come in our journey to heal.

....

Recommended reading: Jean Hall, *Breathe: Simple Breathing Techniques for a Calmer Happier Life*. Eckhart Tolle, *The Power Of Now*. The article "Breathe Like a Tortoise, Live Like a King" by Partha Pratim Bose in The Hindu. Any and all meditations on the Calm app as well as their posts on Instagram.

....

GRIFFIN'S HEART

"When our heart chakra is blocked, we are unable to live at our highest potential. It is important to know that what keeps the flow of energy through the heart stuck is the state of grief. To release this hold on our energy we must practice forgiveness. Forgive, forgive, forgive. Now twerk it like Miley, girl."

~ John San Juan, yoga teacher extraordinaire and pet clothing designer who upcycles high end human clothes @pancakeandgodiva

The Heart Chakra and More Meditation Goodness

I'm a bit of a yoga freak. I just kinda don't get sick of it. And even though you're not really supposed to compare yourself to anyone else while you're practicing, I can freely admit I'm usually the worst one in the class. I wobble out of my postures first, sweat the most and have been known to burst into uncontrollable giggles when I catch sight of myself in the mirror—I tend to resemble an out of shape giraffe trying out for Cirque Du Soleil after a couple of margaritas. But does that matter to me? Nope. I would Chaturanga till the cows come home if they'd let me. There is something about consciously connecting the body and soul to movement and breath that invigorates me to the core and leaves me feeling like a wise old lady who can conquer the world when I'm done.

My favorite teacher from the studio I frequent has taught me a lot more than how to create the perfect triangle pose. He is a sassy Filipino powerhouse named John San Juan. John can inspire me to dig deep into a strength I didn't even know I had, both physically and mentally. His modern day take on Eastern philosophy makes even the most esoteric principles feel relatable; he has this profound way of saying just the thing you needed to hear without even a hint of pretension. And just when you get into a zen state and begin to silently congratulate yourself for feeling "enlightened," he'll crack a filthy joke just to bring you back to Earth and remind you not to take yourself too seriously. You can tell he's wicked smart. Plus he swears a lot which I find disarming and hilarious.

I'm telling you all of this as a disclaimer so that if all this talk of *meditation* and *chakras* feels a bit too *woo-woo* for you, you can know it's still possible to reap the benefits—even without the beaded bracelets and patchouli oil.

I am no spiritual guru. And I have a huge skeptical part of myself that I can feel rolling its eyes when I wander too deeply into all this Eastern philosophical stuff. But I've learned to release some of my stubborn resistance to it and have truly found so much peace by applying parts of it to my life. You can take these ideas and use them literally or metaphorically. Sometimes the imagery alone is enough to get your mind to focus in this helpful way.

Which brings me to the Eastern spiritual tradition of "chakras." John San Juan began talking about these mystical "energy centers" in my Tuesday yoga/meditation class and I've been hooked ever since.

In Anodea Judith's book *Eastern Body, Western Mind: Psychology and the Chakra System as a Path to the Self,* the Eastern chakra system is adapted to the Western framework of Jungian psychology as well as various commonly used modern therapies. The author interprets the structure of each chakra and allows us to apply this knowledge to our individual development.

Chakras are described as energy wheels inside the body. There are seven main chakras and each corresponds with major organs and nerve groups that affect us emotionally and psychologically. Since everything is always moving, each chakra or *energy wheel* needs to be open, aligned, and fluid. If there is a blockage, energy cannot flow. So, if one of the seven chakras is out of balance, the others will inevitably begin to suffer as well. For example, suffering from a feeling of loneliness due to a broken heart could eventually lead to a chronic case of bronchitis, which could lead to anxiety, which could lead to fatigue, and on and on. The idea is to find the *source chakra* and heal that in order to get the others in alignment.

The first three chakras are called The Chakras Of Matter. They are as follows:

First Chakra: Based around the first three vertebrae of the spine. If this chakra is open we feel safe and brave.

Second Chakra: Located between the pubic bone on the belly button. It is the center of creative expression.

Third Chakra: Navel to breast bone. It is the source of personal power.

The fourth chakra connects the first three chakras "Of Matter" to the last three chakras "Of Spirit."

Fourth Chakra: This is the "heart chakra" and serves as a bridge between body, mind, and spirit. It is thought to be incredibly powerful and is our source of love and connection. The heart chakra is the one we will be focusing on the most for our purposes in this book.

The last three chakras "Of Spirit" are as follows:

Fifth Chakra: Throat to mouth (tongue, jaw, and surrounding area). Our source of verbal expression. Our ability to speak our highest truth.

Sixth Chakra: The "third eye chakra," which is right between the eyebrows and is our center for accessing intuition.

Seventh Chakra: Located in the crown of the head, this is our chakra of enlightenment and our connection to whatever we consider to be our "higher-self," or the divine.

The day John San Juan spoke about the heart chakra, something clicked inside of me. It also stung. Perhaps because it resonated so damn much. I put myself in Child's Pose for the last twenty minutes of class and allowed it all to sink in.

He said that the heart chakra is surprisingly not

blocked by anger. It is not blocked by jealousy or greed. What blocks the energy of the heart is *grief*.

Grief. Of course.

And the way out? Well, as my modern day yogic guru John San Juan told me, we can heal grief with the intentional practice of *forgiveness*.

Forgive, forgive, forgive.

Remember, the idea is that the heart chakra is the connection, or the *bridge*, between the physical and psychological, or spiritual. So, if it is out of whack, the list of things that suffer in reaction is long.

Another compelling reminder that we absolutely must learn to grieve properly.

On the next page you'll find a mediation I created to help you access the healing that can come from embracing the visual and emotional notion of the heart chakra. Use it as is or modify as you like.

....

Visit the Griffin's Heart YouTube channel to find my "Heart Clearing Meditation" and other guided meditations and breathing exercises.

....

HEART CLEARING MEDITATION

With one hand on your heart and the other hand on your belly, breath in deeply. The breath that comes in is focused but gentle and directed right around your navel area, where one of your hands is placed. In for seven counts—hold for two beats—then let it flood the heart space for the exhale, another full seven counts. Picture the heart space as a vibrant green light. Do this seven times.

Return to your natural breathing and be still for a few moments.

Now, with the hand that is placed over your heart, feel your heart beating. Listen for it. Can you hear it? Once you're able to sense the beat in the front of your chest, see if you can become aware of it in the back of your rib cage. Try to follow the beat all the way down your torso. The rhythm of it beats like a drum, softly filling your whole body now.

Allow this feeling for as long as you like, continuing to

breathe deeply.

And then silently say the words:

"I forgive you."

Who are you forgiving?

- Yourself
- Someone who needs it
- The feeling of loss that is breaking your heart

Just say the words and allow them to do the work.

Return to the seven-count inhale, two-count hold, and seven-count exhale and repeat three more times. Gently bring your awareness back to your surroundings and end the meditation.

Observe the power that your heart chakra holds—you can find peace in knowing that if you turn your attention to it, you will accept what is, learn forgiveness, and regain a feeling of love.

JOURNAL EXERCISE

Journal your feelings and findings from the Heart Clearing Meditation.

_____

_____

_____

_____

_____

_____

_____

_____

_____

_____

_____

_____

_____

_____

_____

_____

_____

_____

_____

_____

_____

Do you feel a difference in your heart center? In your breathing?

_____

_____

_____

_____

_____

_____

_____

_____

"So if God doesn't give you comfort, what does?"

"Dogs. I believe in dogs."

~ Stephen Colbert talking to Ricky Gervais about his atheism, from *The Late Show with Stephen Colbert*

They Stay Babies Forever

A friend told me that what made the passing of his beautiful parrot, Maggie, so difficult was that she never seemed like an old lady bird. That her end of life suffering just seemed so wrong because of her inherently innocent nature. I could completely relate. Griffin's silliness, sweetness, and anodyne adorableness did not fade with his sick heart. For my friend, Maggie was there and then she wasn't. A baby one day. Gone the next. It seemed especially cruel that this tiny, vibrant Being should suffer.

How do we deal with the feeling that death isn't fair? That the universe has somehow wronged us? Or has made a terrible mistake?

According to Elisabeth Kübler-Ross, a Swiss-American psychiatrist and author of the 1969 book *On Death and Dying*, there are five stages of grief: denial, anger, bargaining, depression, and acceptance. These individual stages can be used as guidelines if we deem them to be helpful, but defining grief in such academic terms can also leave us feeling even less understood. There are not always going to be answers or a framework for how we process feelings. Sometimes it's actually beneficial to just say, "Yes, this *was* unfair," or " Yes, this does just suck." We don't need to *fix* our loss. We just have to survive it. Instead of judging our emotional state, we may be better served to think, "Everything I'm feeling is normal," and then allow ourselves to *just be* exactly as we are. There is no right or wrong in the grief journey—and there is no definite finish line. Death may never feel *fair*. And that is OK. When you love big, the loss will feel big.

JOURNAL EXERCISE

Do you relate to any of Kübler-Ross's five stages of grief: denial, anger, bargaining, depression, and acceptance? If so, which ones seem to fit how you are feeling now (or have felt before)?

_____

_____

_____

Can you imagine yourself transitioning from the way you feel now to something different? What would that be?

_____

_____

Does your grief ebb and flow? Why do you think some days are easier and others are harder?

_____

_____

"Think of intention as the sail of a boat.
Without it there is no movement nor direction.
Set intentions, relax, and trust that the wind
will carry you in the direction you choose."

~ Aaron Doughty, motivational
speaker & metaphysical thinker

Setting Intentions: Allowing Love and Acceptance

Life is beautiful. It is painful. It can be complicated. It has moments of simplicity. All of these facets add to its intricate experience.

Our animals are here for a short time (relative to us) so how do we accept that the ache we feel when they leave is worth the gifts they give us while they are here? My answer is to not run from the uncomfortable feeling of pain, but instead to acknowledge that it's just part of the complex beauty that is life.

There is huge power and strength in acceptance. In allowing yourself to be vulnerable and realizing that there is no real answer, no absolute resolve. By honoring your pain, your grief can transform. Your heart can open and you can renew.

There is a part of you that will *always* hold onto your Being, that amazing life that has only left in physical form. You can learn to work *with* that new part, or against it.

Who will you be once you *allow* yourself to soften and

grow with this feeling of loss? When you allow healing with the *intention* of love and acceptance, you can go forward with much more wisdom and strength so that your loss can be handled with grace and feel more peaceful.

Setting daily intentions that align us with our ultimate goal of living a happy, successful life can put us back on track when we're lost in grief. Intentions give us purpose and motivation.

....

Recommended Reading: Bruce Black, *Writing Yoga: A Guide to Keeping a Practice Journal.*

....

EXERCISE

See how many of these intentions you can incorporate into your day today.

Set the intention to do something that makes you laugh today.

Set the intention to find someone, online or in person, who understands how you are feeling and set aside a reasonable amount of time to talk.

Set the intention to meditate this morning (and every morning for a week!).

Set the intention to exercise. Go for a walk, do yoga, play tennis—whatever gets those endorphins flowing.

Set the intention to allocate time for mourning, time for active remembering, and time for living.

. . . . . .

JOURNAL EXERCISE

How did you do with setting intentions? It can take time to reap the rewards. Journal about how it went for you.

_____

_____

_____

_____

_____

_____

_____

_____

_____

_____

_____

_____

_____

_____

_____

_____

_____

_____

_____

_____

_____

_____

_____

_____

_____

_____

_____

_____

_____

_____

_____

_____

_____

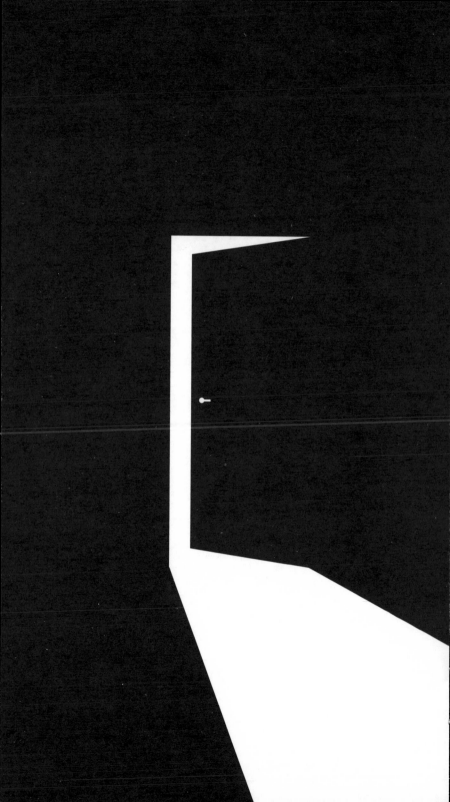

Go *through* the darkness to get back into the light

JED THE HUMANOID

Grandaddy, The Sophtware Slump

Last night something pretty bad happened
We lost a friend (we lost a friend)
All shocked and broken (all shocked and broken)
Shutdown exploded (shutdown exploded)

Jed could run or walk, sing or talk and,
Compile thoughts and (compile thoughts and)
Solve lots of problems (solve lots of problems)
We learned so much from him (learned so much from him)

Music Therapy

The place where I can truly "feel" in the purest way is through music. Certain songs allowed me to feel the spirit of Griffin so completely that it was as if he'd found a secret channel to let me know he was still right there by my side.

My husband listened to a song called "Jed the Humanoid" by a band called Grandaddy that would make him think of Griffin. It brought him peace and put him in a mood of gratitude. He listened to that song quite a bit. We even named our next animal—a fluffy white dog—"Jed" because of it (see 'How Your Being Got Her/His Name' on page 109).

Music therapy has been used for centuries to heal. Neuroscientists Robert J. Zatorre and Valorie N. Salimpoor wrote a *New York Times* article "Why Music Makes Our Brain Sing," about the strong connections made between a mere sequence of sounds (aka a song) and the reward system in the brain. The explanation for this is actually pretty cool. Studies show that music stimulates all areas of the brain, and when our brain has the "appropriate" response to musical stimuli the striatum releases a chemical known as dopamine as its reward. Dopamine has been referred to as a "motivation molecule" and can result in a feeling of pleasure, preservation, and euphoria. Pharmaceutical companies are raking in a fortune by making little synthetic pills that increase our dopamine production—but music encourages the natural release of this chemical. Music therapy has been successful in treating various neurological disorders because melody, rhythm, and other musical elements enhance neuroplasticity in the brain. "Neuroplasticity" refers to our brain's natural ability to change and adapt by forming new connections.

If music is a productive treatment for neurological disorders like ADHD and Parkinson's, it is easy to see how it can be just as effective when dealing with grief.

For my whole life, music has been one of my greatest passions. I have studied and collected music intensely since I was seven years old—I even ended up going to college for it. While my high school peers would be out partying with friends on a Saturday night, I would be holed up in my bedroom dissecting a song note by note. After reading Daniel J. Levitin's book *This Is Your Brain On Music* I was able to grasp the science behind my own musical obsession. Music has an almost magical ability to take us out of our emotional environment, a healthy escape from sadness—and, of course, our brains love this feeling. We take pleasure in making predictions about what is coming next. In being able to *foresee*. And when we're buried in our sadness, our loss, being able to see a light at the end of the tunnel, fueled by our natural "happy chemical" dopamine, well, that is a very good thing.

A song that resonates with us, whether through melody or lyrics, can help us confront our emotions in a powerful way. It can provide a vehicle to reminisce, aid with visualization, and put us into an almost ethereal state. Music is a creative way to focus our attention and connect us to an array of coping techniques.

All that to say—bring on the dopamine. Go find your healing song.

MY HEALING SONG

Song title: _____

Artist: _____

Favorite lyric: _____

_____

_____

_____

_____

Here's a poem written by Canadian actress and writer, and my friend, Kate Hewlett. Her dog Dudley was rescued from Ohio where apparently he'd been used for target practice—although you'd never know it from his happy demeanor. Dudley was a hunk of a black lab mix who died peacefully while eating cheese and listening to Joni Mitchell. He'll be missed forever.

A Poem for Dudley

awkward paws and velvet ears
changed my life in just five years
got my license just for you
moved three times to suit your mood
shady past and rocky start
puked on adam, won his heart
friends with squirrels pigs and sheep
only barked when fast asleep
meningitis, UTIs
ear infections droopy eyes
bullets in your hips and chest
still so trusting, still the best
thought that every car was mine
every hour was dinner time
awkward paws and velvet ears
what I'd give for five more years

~ Kate Hewlett, actress and writer

CREATIVITY EXERCISE

If you feel inspired to do so, you can write your own poem or song, or include your own illustration, painting, or drawing here:

Space for creativity

Space for creativity

Space for creativity

"The intuitive mind is a sacred gift, and the rational mind is a faithful servant. We have created a society that honors the servant and has forgotten the gift."

~ Albert Einstein

Art Therapy

The Nobel Prize winning neuropsychologist and neurobiologist Dr. Roger W. Sperry characterized the brain as having two parts—the *left* hemisphere being the verbal and rational part that thinks in numbers and letters, labelling, and organizing, and the *right* hemisphere, the non-verbal, more perceptual part that interprets things as "a whole."

In Dr. Betty Edwards' book *Drawing On The Right Side Of The Brain* she proposes that if we can learn ways to bypass the left hemisphere of our brain, we can access the less dominant right hemisphere and tap into a more creative, intuitive part of who we are. She specifically uses this philosophy to teach people how to draw.

If your mind is shouting at you now saying something like "No way! I'm NOT an artist and I'm not doing this dumb exercise," then that is a perfect example of your "left brain" taking over and precisely why this exercise may be beneficial. Remember, the left side is used for analyzing, language processing, calculating—skills that seem to be valued in society. But as Dr. Edwards teaches us, finding ways to tap into our right brain can bring us leaps of insight where things just seem to fall into place. We can experience a bit of reprieve from the racing thoughts that often bombard us when we are in emotional pain (especially when experiencing loss). Perhaps we may even discover a creativity we never knew was there.

All of this sounds pretty therapeutic to someone deep in grief.

GRIFFIN'S HEART

UPSIDE DOWN DRAWING OF YOUR PET

Find a photo you love of your Being. Then flip the photo so it is upside down. Grab a sharp pencil and an eraser and use the page provided in this book. Now instead of mentally labelling, "I'm now drawing an ear, now I'm drawing the nose, etc." and then commenting to yourself, "that doesn't even look like an ear! I'm terrible at drawing, etc." Just focus on the lines and contours- drawing what you actually see rather than what you think. The upside-down mode should quiet your left brain from categorizing parts of your pet's features and allow you to just see them as abstract shapes and shadows that are easy to mimic. When you are done, feel free to add color, or more shading before you look at it right side up and take it in.

AFTER THE EXERCISE

How's your drawing? A realistic resemblance? Or more impressionistic? Hopefully you were able to let go and enjoy the process a little. Maybe you even created something that you're proud of along the way—honoring your Being by accessing your artistic streak.

How to Get Unstuck on 'Why'

Tormenting ourselves with 'why' questions keeps us stuck in the worst part of grief. Some 'why' questions play on repeat in our brains and of course, many don't have satisfactory answers. The brain loves repetition and so the why's continue like a playlist set to repeat and we get more and more lost in them.

Why questions like:

Why did this happen to me?
Why did my Being die so young?
Why did she/he have to suffer?
Why didn't I do more to prevent it?

The challenge here is to flip the dialogue. Accept that most of these 'why's' likely won't ever be answered and gently change those 'why's' to 'how's.' There's a subtle but powerful difference in shifting the dialogue to 'how' that can be helpful.

How questions could be:

How can I find ways to cope?
How can I honor my Being's memory?
How can I refocus my negative thought patterns?
How can I allow myself to be vulnerable again?

These 'how' questions have answers. These answers will evolve over time and you may be able to witness your healing progress when answering them.

....

Recommended Reading: Sue Morris and Dana Farber, *The Psychology of Grief—Applying Cognitive and Behaviour Therapy Principles*, via the Australian Psychological Society.

....

JOURNAL EXERCISE

How can you cope with your feeling of loss? Write down at least one coping technique to try.

_____

_____

_____

_____

_____

_____

How can you honor your Being's memory?

_____

_____

_____

_____

_____

How can you shift any persistent negative thought patterns to ones that foster good feelings like love and gratitude?

_____

_____

_____

_____

_____

_____

How can you allow yourself to be vulnerable again after experiencing a sharp and painful loss? How will you keep your heart open enough to allow another animal (or person) in?

_____

_____

_____

_____

_____

_____

Space for photo

PART III

TO SAY GOODBYE

"When all is said and done,
We will be remembered by
how hard we loved."

~ The Better Man Project

The End of Life (Ain't Pretty)

The end of life is just not pretty. There's no way around it. Even when we think we're prepared, that it is our Being's *time to go,* just seeing the animal that we love suffer in those last moments can leave a tragic and indelible imprint on the mind.

But the end is usually, hopefully, such a small part of the big, beautiful picture.

So what can we do to reconcile all of our feelings about the end—how it happened, the circumstances surrounding it, the decisions we made, or the mental images that stick inside the brain?

It comes back to deliberately choosing your thoughts. Actively *choose* to accept that the end was only one part of a whole life. When your thoughts turn to you and your Being's last moments together, spend one minute on them if you need to and then return to the love.

Can you do that?

Go ahead and acknowledge your painful memory of

the end when it comes up but always have a wonderful memory in your pocket at the ready to replace it with. What I'm suggesting is actually what my own therapist had me practice. This is a common Cognitive Behavioral Therapy (CBT) technique, something you can practice on your own.

Here are a couple examples of painful thoughts and suggestions for new, more productive, healing thoughts to replace them with:

Thought:
"I wasn't even there for his last moments! He must have felt abandoned. My poor guy..."

Thought:
"She was in so much pain at the end. I wish I had taken her to the vet sooner."

Acknowledge:
"Yes. That is tragic. I can breathe into that pain and acknowledge the feeling of regret. It's real."

AND...
What is also there are the seven years before that and many hundreds of amazing memories to call upon. For example:

"I traveled across the country by car so he wouldn't have to fly (his heart wasn't strong enough). I'd stop and feed him ice cream along the way, which he loved. My husband thought I was nuts but went along with it because he knew how much I loved him."

Our thoughts create our feelings, and therefore, our reality. And when we can grasp that we alone are in control of what we think, we realize that any unwanted thoughts—ones that may be playing on a loop—can be changed. We can choose positive memories in favor of the ones that are breaking our hearts.

We can reframe the whole darn thing.

Acknowledge the end, sure, but then always go back to the love.

JOURNAL EXERCISE

Identify a persistent thought that has been on 'repeat' since the loss of your Being that is causing you pain and write it down.

_____

_____

_____

_____

_____

Now acknowledge and honor your feelings—they are real and valid. Write down how this persistent thought makes you feel.

_____

_____

_____

_____

_____

And finally, write down 1-3 more positive thoughts or memories you can have at the ready to counter the thought that is causing pain.

1. _____
_____
_____
_____

2. _____
_____
_____
_____

3. _____
_____
_____
_____

Oy, the Guilt.

A little bit of guilt, for the right reasons, can be healthy. Next time, we'll vaccinate; next time, we won't feed the pet bones or scraps. Next time, we'll consult the vet immediately about that odd behavior change. A lot of guilt, however, is not so healthy. Left unchecked, it can prevent us from seeking the joy of a new pet—and even ruin our lives. I've spoken with pet owners who have suffered from guilt for years. So if you can't shake the sense of being "to blame" for your loss, you could be in for a long, rough ride—unless you choose to change direction. Notice that I said "choose." **While we can't always control how we feel, we can control how to respond to those emotions. We can choose whether to control those emotions, or whether to allow them to control us.**

~ *"Breaking the Power of Guilt"* by Moira Anderson Allen M.Ed. via *The Pet Loss Support Page.*

If this chapter is not relevant to you—if you feel like guilt, of any kind, does not apply to you—then count yourself lucky and please skip ahead.

In my own story, and in hearing countless other

people's stories on losing their pets, the subject of guilt seems to come up over and over again:

- Guilt for feeling like you didn't do enough
- Guilt for not being able to hold your pet in their last moments
- Guilt for feeding them the wrong food
- Guilt for traveling too much
- Guilt for not noticing that there was something wrong
- Guilt for deciding to end their suffering

Guilt, guilt, guilt. And more guilt.

I had a ton of it. Even as I write this today, years later, I still feel that familiar pang in my heart. It might be the hardest part to heal. These incredible Beings *depend* on us. But they can't tell us when they are sick and we often don't notice that something is wrong soon enough. Busy schedules, the demands of work and family, and other reasonable priorities may mean we often just cannot meet every need the way we'd like to.

Sadly, it's all too common for feelings of guilt to eclipse the memory of our many sacrifices, all the effort and love we gave—the good that came before the end.

It is so important not to let that happen.

There was life before death. And you probably wouldn't be reading this book right now if you hadn't loved the heck out of that Being. Remember that. Hold onto that.

JOURNAL EXERCISE

WHY do you feel guilty? What do you feel you may have done wrong? This writing exercise may feel very difficult. Be brave. No matter what happened, there is a path to self-forgiveness. Let it out.

_____

_____

_____

_____

_____

_____

_____

_____

_____

_____

_____

_____

OK. That's done.

Maybe you actually made mistakes. Maybe you didn't. Maybe it will never be clear.

Animals are tricky. They can't give us the answers. All we can do is love them while they're here. We have to release the rest.

So, you're allowed to feel bad this one last time. Feel it. Feel it big.

And now...

LET. IT. GO.

Return to the love. The love is what it's all about anyway.

JOURNAL EXERCISE

Name three things you did to show love.

_____

_____

_____

_____

_____

_____

_____

_____

_____

_____

_____

_____

_____

_____

_____

Ho'oponopono

I love you,
I'm sorry,
please forgive me,
thank you.

~ Hawaiian Ho'oponopono saying

There is a Hawaiian healing practice of forgiveness called Ho'oponopono. It was used to restore peace with ancestors, with living relations, and within. The translation of the word is to put right, shape, correct, revise, amend, or rectify.

It is thought to be cleansing and can have mysterious and even miraculous effects. It's very simple and can be used on a specific issue ("I want freedom from the guilt I feel for not being there when my animal had her last moments") or something more general ("Seeing my animal at the end of his life has filled me with such sadness that I couldn't help him").

You just say the words: "I love you. I'm sorry. Please forgive me. Thank you." They don't even have to be in that exact order. When I practice Ho'oponopono, I imagine my Griffin saying back: "I love you too, it's OK, you are forgiven" and "you are welcome." Few grief techniques are as elegant in their simplicity and practice.

GRIFFIN'S HEART

Lessons Learned

Animals have taught me so much. They have taught me that love's boundaries extend far beyond language. That play and cuddles are often enough. How greeting someone enthusiastically *every single time* they walk through the door is both hilarious and lovesome, and we should all feel adored that way sometimes.

Love is a mirror. It serves as a reflection that we can learn from if we allow ourselves to honestly look with awareness. The love I have for my son is always showing me the parts of myself that I need to improve—patience and staying present, to name a few. The love I have for my friends is constantly evolving to show me just what I price my worthiness at, and because of this I've gotten better and better at choosing who I let in my life. And the way I love my animals has shown me that I have a deep desire to be loved unconditionally. Exploring all the reasons 'why' can be very illuminating.

Griffin taught me more specific lessons, too. I used

to watch him and think, "Wow, you'll know my children someday." But at just seven years old, Griffin died much earlier than he should have. He never met our beautiful son, Milo. He never got to live in our new home with the enclosed backyard and bask in the sun all day like I wanted him to.

He showed me how a short life is still a beautiful life. That you can never, ever know what's around the corner so you must live with purpose.

These things are ingrained in me now.

JOURNAL EXERCISE

What are some lessons your Being taught you?

_____

_____

_____

_____

_____

_____

_____

_____

_____

_____

_____

_____

_____

_____

_____

_____

"Our body is just a vehicle for us while we're here. It is our soul and our spirit that last forever."

~ Brian L. Weiss, author of
Many Lives, Many Masters

Afterlife: Energy Can Neither Be Created Nor Destroyed

I grew up in a Jewish home, but my experience was much more about culture than religious beliefs. I can count on one hand the times we went to Temple, and the sound of my stepmom snoring through those few services will resonate forever in my eardrums. My father was, and still is, openly agnostic. Needless to say, I was never given a blueprint for what an afterlife might look like, or taught that there even was one. And yet, somehow I have always been a relentless spiritual seeker—searching for proof that there is something beyond the tangible. Some place that comes after the suffering.

In *Women Food And God*, Geneen Roth writes, "*I don't believe in the God with long white hair and X-ray vision that favors some people, some countries, some religions and not others. I don't believe in the sky dweller, the knower of all things, the granter of the prayers. But I do believe in the world beyond appearances and that there is so much we can't see or touch or know just by looking. And I do believe—because I have experienced it again and again— that the world beyond appearances is as real as a chair, a dog, a teapot."*

There have been moments in my life where I have been left stunned by mysterious synchronicities—and others where I have felt abandoned and hopeless—only to be guided back to wellness by an energy so powerful and profound, that even my most cynical notions couldn't extinguish my lingering sense of divinity. My seven-year-old son has always had an unexplainable, deep intuition about spirituality. He's explained to me that there is absolutely a Source Energy that we all have easy access to. He says that it lives in your heart and that some people call it "God," but he prefers to call it "Love." He has also told me that when we die the part of us that's connected to "Love" lives on, but in a different world. One we cannot see yet.

This is the same kid who refuses to believe in the Tooth Fairy.

Where is he getting this from?

Elizabeth Lesser talks about a *spiritual longing* in her book *The Seeker's Guide* where she describes a yearning to understand our place within the mystery of the universe. She says this *longing* "is as ancient and as instinctual as our other basic human needs." I can definitely relate— I've twisted in the gravitational pull of the big existential questions and strained to answer the unanswerable since I was old enough to recognize my reflection in a mirror. There is a natural, albeit frustrating, dichotomy that occurs when you've been raised with no real religious constitution but are determined to lean into spiritual hunches. I'm deeply envious of people whose faith is so strong it leaves no doubt that there is a heaven out there—a well-defined afterlife. Because wouldn't that be amazing? To be reunited with our loved ones? The idea of this is just too hard to pass up.

The one idea that seems to satisfy both my science-based upbringing as well as my "spiritual longing" is the law of physics and chemistry called "**The Law Of Conservation Of Energy.**"* It states that energy can neither be created nor destroyed; rather, it can only be transformed or transferred from one form to another.

Physicist Aaron Freeman said to NPR, "*You want a physicist to speak at your funeral. You want the physicist to talk to your grieving family about the conservation of energy, so they will understand that your energy has not died. You want the physicist to remind your sobbing mother about the first law of thermodynamics; that no energy gets created in the universe, and none is destroyed.*"*

Now, wouldn't this *law* mean that the energy that was my sweet Griffin—and that of every other loved one who's passed on—*has* to exist somewhere else? I mean, isn't that the proof that some way, somehow we are never really gone?

Look, I'm just stating the law y'all!

When an animal dies, it is not just their physical form that we miss. It is their energy. Their *Being* as Eckhart Tolle said. And that is not lost. Even a spiritual-seeking skeptic like myself can learn to embrace this concept.

If I close my eyes and focus my thoughts I can *feel* Griffin's energy. His sparkly little light. The inexplicable essence of what made him, him.

And, yes, maybe this is a coping mechanism. Maybe it's just a crutch to help me make sense of a pain that needs a happy ending. But I'm an open-minded, spiritual yearner. And accepting that Griffin's energy is still alive and well feels damn good.

Plus, who am I to break the law?

....

Recommended reading: Aaron Freeman, *Conservation Of Energy Wikipedia, Eulogy From a Physicist.*

....

JOURNAL EXERCISE

Does the idea that your animal, your "Being," is living on in some form of an afterlife bring you peace? If so, close your eyes, take a few deep breaths, and really let yourself feel their energy. Imagine that you will be reunited one day. Sit in that feeling as long as you like. Write about any special observations.

_____

_____

_____

_____

_____

_____

_____

_____

_____

_____

_____

_____

"Gratitude has the power to shift everything."

~ Unknown

A Thank You Note

Some of us are rampant thank you note writers. Whether it's to acknowledge the thirteen ladies who helped plan your perfect baby-shower or that friend who was there for you when you needed them most—taking time out of your day to express true gratitude can leave both giver and receiver feeling recognized and complete.

Before my son was born I was pretty prolific about it. I'd pull out the specialty papers, glitter pens, and stickers and go to town, gleeful as a third grader, saying my "merci beaucoups" from the bottom of my type-A heart. After my son... not so much. I just wasn't great at managing my time while I figured out how to manage his. These thank you notes can sometimes take hours! And I just stopped prioritizing them.

But as the years went by, I kind of started to miss it. Something just seemed less *special* without taking time to contemplate what someone's gifts, material or emotional, meant to me. So, recently I've taken it up again and I have to say, it feels pretty darn good to fully take in someone else's kindness. Or effort. Or love. And then, somehow, it feels even better to release that feeling back to whomever deserves it, in a flow of genuine gratitude. It's a relatively easy way to put the twinkle back in life.

Showing deep appreciation is like an electric two-way street. The epitome of give and take. It's like, if a boomerang embodied the vibration of love and healing. You get the picture.

I believe in the power of gratitude. Dare I say it's the secret to happiness.

JOURNAL EXERCISE

Let's write a thank you note directly to your Being. Allow yourself to see how good it feels to reflect upon everything they did for you. The energy behind that is powerful and can only do positive things.

_____

_____

_____

_____

_____

_____

_____

_____

_____

_____

_____

_____

Hold on to what is good
even if it is a handful of earth.

Hold on to what you believe
even if it is a tree which stands by itself.

Hold on to life
even when it is easier letting go.

Hold on to my hand (my paw)
even when I have gone away from you.

~ Native American prayer

Memorializing Your Being

Considering I am surrounded by an animal-loving family and pet-obsessed friends, it's interesting that I have yet to attend one single pet funeral or memorial service. I have been to countless human ceremonial send-offs, but not a single one for friends or family who have lost their beloved Being. Why is that?

When Griffin died, giving him a funeral never even crossed my mind. We had him cremated by a company my vet recommended and that beige, mediocre box that contains his ashes has sat on my vanity ever since. But Griffin was anything but beige. And somewhere deep inside I knew that he deserved a better goodbye.

Years later, my beautiful sixteen-year-old cat, Cleo, happened to die on my husband's fortieth birthday. I reluctantly made the decision *not* to cancel the party I'd been planning for him with our closest friends. It felt a bit strange at first and I was a snivelling mess, but it turned out to be a day I will cherish forever. My friends came with flowers and cards and the event morphed into a beautiful mashup celebration of Cleo's life and my husband's milestone birthday. That day brought me a sense of closure that I didn't experience with Griffin. When the inevitable happens again, some sort of ceremony or memorial will *unapologetically* be part of my grieving process and honoring a life lived.

....

You can check out the photos from this impromptu memorial day on our @GriffinsHeartBook Instagram page.

....

Different cultures and religions specifically honor their lost pets in some pretty interesting and beautiful ways and you might be surprised to learn that the pet funeral industry is in fact thriving all over the world. There are approximately 750 pet cemeteries in the US alone.

I read a story about the Westchester County Hartsdale Pet Cemetery, one of the world's oldest burial places for animals, where Rev. David James provides funeral services to animals for people of different faiths. In his service he points out that the loss of a pet can be as devastating as the loss of people in our lives. He says, "It's emotionally healthy to participate in a memorial service and to say goodbye to the wonderful animals that have brought joy and comfort." Different cultures from around the world have developed traditions to help them find peace in saying goodbye.

What follows are some ideas, inspiration, and considerations that you can use if, and only if, you decide that a send-off ceremony feels right to you.

Guest List: Who will you invite? Will it be just you? Family? What about a close friend? Share your memorial with the people that you love and trust.

Venue: This can be as simple or as elaborate as you like. You can rent a space or find a pet funeral parlor if that suits your wants/needs. But your living room or backyard would work perfectly as well. If you're doing this at home pick a small intimate area to decorate and place a few special things.

Special Things: Place a favorite dish, collar, bed, or toy. If you have an urn or a plaster paw print, include those.

Photo/Art: Place a small photo with your special objects. If you are an artist or craftsperson, do a painting or create a sculpture for the event.

Candles: Candlelight is soft and intimate. Place some candles in and around your venue for atmosphere. Don't burn down your house.

Flowers: Flowers are nature's amazing gift and make any occasion feel special. Fill your venue with wild flowers or pick a single rose. You can't go wrong.

Thank You Note: Write a thank you note to your Being and read it aloud. Tell them what they meant to you and what you will miss. Remember to thank them for your time together.

Tell a Story: Share a funny or memorable story about your Being. Write it down and read it aloud if you need to. Let others prepare a story, too.

Prayers: There are beautiful prayers in some cultures and religions that you may wish to incorporate into your ceremony.

For example, the Sikh nighttime prayer of peace "Kirtan Sohila" says, *"Day after day, He cares for His beings; the Great Giver watches over all"* and *"you shall dwell in peace."*

Or for Jewish pets, there is a beautiful prayer from the reconstructural prayer book series *Kol Haneshama: Shabbat Eve* by Rabbi David A Teutsch. The prayer says, *"Pour upon us your love, lift us up in our sorrow, and keep us on the path of companionship and loyalty that our animals have taught us."*

"A Christian Prayer for a Dead Pet" * reads, *"Eternal Father, we bring you our grief in the loss of (name of pet) and ask for courage to bear it. We bring you our thanks for (name of pet) who lived among us and gave us freely of his/her love. We commit our friend and companion (name of pet) into your loving hands. Give us eyes to see how your love embraces all creatures and every living thing speaks to us of your love. Amen."*

Donation: Give to an animal charity or rescue group.

Set out a bowl and ask everyone to make a small donation. Turn the death of your Being into an opportunity to help another.

Music: Play a special song. Pick one that resonates with your Being's essence. Ask everyone to stay silent while you listen, remember, and process everything that is happening.

....

Please share something from your ceremony on our Instagram page @GriffinsHeartBook.

....

Recommeded Reading: Karen Iris Tucker, "Sitting Shiva For Spot" from Forward Magazine, Saintland.com "Prayer For Pets".

....

**"There are all kinds of love
in this world but never the
same love twice."**

~ F Scott Fitzgerald

"Hope and fear cannot occupy the same space. Invite one to stay."

~ Maya Angelou

Hope

In no way do I intend to rush you, or even encourage you to find another Being to adopt into your life. You may not be ready, and that is completely OK.

Just don't be afraid of the pain.

Sometimes in our many layers of grief it's hard to invite hope in. Hope is the feeling we get when we start to accept the basic truth that life is *meant* to be lived with joy. That it is a simple choice we can all make. It doesn't mean that painful memories won't pop up from time to time. But we can learn to trust, without demanding answers, that things will get easier. Because they will.

My wish is that this book has helped you see that the good is so much stronger, so much more *relevant* than the bad. That the end was just a small piece of a broad and beautiful life. I hope you truly see that there is nothing to feel guilty about now. An animal's heart is perfectly pure and they would unequivocally *want* you to be happy. And safe. And loved.

And trust me—if and when you *do* decide to adopt a new animal—you are not replacing *anybody*. Don't even try it. No two animals are alike. No two loves are alike. A new animal is a brand new adventure. You will know when it's right.

We can activate hope when we decide to believe we are worthy of living in the present rather than the past.

Hope is about the best choice you can make when things are feeling rough. I'm a big fan of hope.

JOURNAL EXERCISE

What is your hope for yourself right now?

_____

_____

_____

_____

_____

_____

_____

What hope would you imagine your Being would want for you?

_____

_____

_____

_____

_____

Any other thoughts? Get it out here...

_____

_____

_____

_____

_____

_____

_____

_____

_____

_____

_____

_____

_____

_____

_____

_____

_____

_____

_____

The risk of love is loss.

The price of loss is grief.

But the pain of grief is only a shadow when compared with the pain of never risking love.

~ Hilary Stanton Zunin

Who will you become?

When people adore their pets, a part of me connects to them automatically. We may not have one other molecule of common ground in our bodies, minds or spirits—But if you treat your animal like family and are a devoted caregiver, we can possibly be friends for life. I recognize something in pet-lovers that feels comforting and familiar to me. I've come to believe that this is because *we are a certain kind of tribe that seeks out joy, light, and connection.*

Life, too often, has us trudging along our own individual paths wearing heavy boots. Getting weighed down by pain. But when we choose to share our heart with an animal, we find an innocent way to distract from those difficult feelings. Our sweet Being becomes a mighty sponge, absorbing the hardest parts—holding our hurt for us with a selflessness few humans can ever own.

So when they die, what then? The light goes off. The joy goes missing.

But it doesn't have to be that way.

Psychotherapist, Lori Gottlieb writes in her memoir *Maybe You Should Talk to Someone* "*What are we so afraid of? It's not as if we are going to peer in those darker corners, flip on the light, and find a bunch of cockroaches. Fireflies love the dark, too. There's beauty in those places. But we have to look in there to see it.*"

After all of the unconditional love, the fun, the acceptance—our animals have given us one last gift. They've given us an *opportunity*. An opportunity to grow and expand our hearts—our own *Beings*.

Losing an animal doesn't have to be something that we are required to simply "get over." The old way of dealing with death feels antiquated and lacks a certain integrity. But we have the ability to change the ***culture of grief***. Grief is an active emotion that we can choose to observe and tend to. Where we used to be encouraged to brush aside our painful feelings—dismiss them and pretend they aren't really there—now we know that we have the option to examine them. To explore them. We can sit in a bit of discomfort and figure out why we loved that specific Being so much. What does it say about them? What does it say about us?

I want to look forward only *after* I've looked back. After I've learned everything I needed to learn and cleared any lingering negative energy or regret that may be surreptitiously lurking in the shadows.

Through emotional exploration, community and love—we can get back to the light. The kind that changes us for the better. That is what can happen when we are honest about what we've gone through. When we allow ourselves to love to our full capacity and honor the importance of losing someone who meant the world to us. This is where we grow.

....

Find your community with us at @GriffinsHeartthebook on Instagram. Let's support each other.

....

Epilogue

Sept. 5th, 2005

I was away on business when Griffin died. My absence at the end contributed to the guilt that enveloped me for so long. It was September 5th when my husband, Kelcey, called me from the animal hospital to tell me that a blood clot had moved into my poor cat's brain—an ugly complication from his cardiomyopathy. I knew in my bones that he had been through enough. The idea of him suffering for even one more second was not an option— and it outweighed any idea that he should wait for me to find a flight home so I could say goodbye in the flesh.

"No more pain for you," I thought.

Kelcey sat under the cold fluorescent lights at the animal clinic with Griffin curled up on his lap. He was wrapped in his favorite pink beaded blanket and had the only toy he ever really cared about, a green crunchy frog, pressed up to his skin.

Griffin had been mine five years before I ever met my husband but he stole the hearts of everyone who met him. And my husband was no exception. We sat there on the phone with thousands of miles between us and cried harder than we've cried since.

My husband put the phone up to Griffin's ear so I could tell him goodbye. It all seemed so cheap and unfair considering how Griffin had been there for me through so much. He'd always made coming home easier after a terrible day—always made me feel completely loved even if it felt like the whole world was rejecting me. He'd given me consistency, where I'd had none. And now I was abandoning him when he finally needed me back.

I was so sorry. I whispered it over and over into what I felt like was the air. Kelcey told me that in all of Griffin's pain and confusion, he still managed to lift his face and nuzzle it to the phone. To this day, he tells me this was the truth. My last living connection to him.

And of course, there is no conclusion to loss. There is no mathematical equation that solves the pain. But there is comfort in support. There is bravery that develops from facing grief head on. And then, finally, there is wisdom that emerges from everything we learn along the way.

In learning all of this, little by little, I did begin to heal. Eventually, I didn't feel the need to focus on the hardest parts of losing Griffin. I know that this was because I'd unearthed everything that needed to be exposed. I learned to focus on the good and gently release the bad. I had shone a light into every shadowy corner, down the darkest hallways, exposed my grief for what it was and made peace with my regrets. I started to find solace in the things I'd done right.

And now I have this book. Dedicated to the heart that was both completely pure and also riddled with disease. The tiny muscle that was Griffin's heart ended up being just as mysterious as he was to me. Too beautiful and poetic to stay a mere earthling forever. Perhaps I'm romanticizing—but, you know, I just don't think so. He was seven years old when he died. In that short time he gave me an understanding of love that cannot be replaced. I don't ever want to feel removed enough from him to forget our special connection, even if that sometimes causes me discomfort or pain.

And maybe nothing I write could ever truly articulate what that little feline angel meant to me. But by honoring and remembering him—*sharing* the impact he had on me with *you*—perhaps that's my best shot giving him the farewell he deserves.

This is Griffin's story. And I hope your Being's story now lives inside these pages too.

With compassion and love, I thank you for letting me take this journey with you.

~ Reagan Pasternak

THE END

Acknowledgements

Kelcey Parker, Griffin's Heart simply wouldn't exist without you. I tried to give up on this endeavor multiple times. I had countless temper tantrums and self-defeating conversations—but you were having none of it. You knew I needed to write this book. Thank you for knowing me and believing in me. You are everything. Thank you to my editors, Nyei Murez, Daniel Johnson and Pam Alster-Jahrmakt. You guys are absolute pros. Pam, I'm so impressed with your brilliant brain. Your guidance and expertise was a game-changer. Thank you to Kate Hewlett and Erin Karpluk for contributing your precious tributes. To David Crabb and Katie Featherston for being the first people to hear what I'd written down. It was terrifying to share Griffin's Heart, especially at such a raw stage, and I'm not sure that you know how much your advice helped me move forward. Anna Silk, your genuine encouragement and love of the material has given me so much courage. How did you get so generous? Andles, this book is also dedicated to you. I love you and I'm grateful for all of the passion you have for animal wellness—you matter a lot. To the authors of every book cited and quote listed. Thank you for educating me and inspiring me. My mass consumption of books has actually amounted to something! Thank you to Dad and Cele for your constant encouragement—I'm so lucky to have always had your uncompromising support. I'm so lucky to have your uncompromising support. To Cortney, Debbie and Steve—I love you guys forever. I'm so grateful I got to read excerpts of Griffin's Heart to my sweet momma in the months before she died. She was a true poet and I'm so lucky to have a small part of that inside of me. I feel you with me every single day, Momma. Thank you to the countless people, often complete strangers, who expressed their sorrow to me after losing an animal— your vulnerability kept me focused and on purpose.

GRIFFIN'S HEART